HOW TO EXCEL AS A REAL ESTATE WEALTHCRAFT PROFESSIONAL

THE 9 NUGGETS OF A REAL ESTATE PRO

The Realtors Publishers

Contents

INTRODUCTION

Welcome to" ***How to Excel as a Real Estate Wealthcraft Professional***" your comprehensive companion to learning the art and wisdom of real estate success. In this perceptive trip, we claw into the foundations of erecting wealth through canny real estate practices. From decoding request trends to executing effective negotiation, this book is your roadmap to creating a flourishing property portfolio.

Explore the complications of legal considerations, upgrade your customer operation chops, and discover innovative marketing strategies acclimatized for the dynamic real estate geography. This book not only equips you with the tools for immediate success but also emphasizes the significance of ethical conduct in sustaining long-term substance.

Whether you are a seasoned realtor or a budding professional, unleash the secrets to getting a Real Estate Wealthcraft Professional and pave your way to lasting success in the dynamic world of real estate.

CHAPTER 1

Foundations of Real Estate Wealthcraft

Welcome to the foundation of your trip toward excellence in the realm of real estate. In this foundational chapter, we lay the root for your success as a Real Estate Wealthcraft Professional.

1. Understanding the Terrain

Embark on a comprehensive disquisition of the ever-evolving real estate geography. Navigate through request dynamics, relating trends, and learning the art of anticipating shifts in property values. Your capability to interpret the terrain is the compass that will guide you to profitable openings.

2. Casting Your Expertise

Artificer in real estate is further than just deals, it's about honing your chops to a position of mastery. Dive deep into the complications of property evaluation, investment analysis, and threat operation. Learn to carve your moxie, icing you stand out in a competitive request.

3. Building A Solid Foundation

Just as a sturdy foundation supports a towering structure, your real estate career requires a solid base. Uncover the principles of fiscal knowledge and strategic planning. We will guide you in constructing a flexible foundation that can ride request oscillations and propel you toward sustained success.

By the end of the posterior chapters, you will not only grasp the fundamentals of real estate but also be equipped with the tools to forge ahead with confidence. Get ready to make your wealthcraft with perfection and purpose. The tour has just begun, and the attainableness is measureless.

CHAPTER 2

Mastering Market Analysis and Trends

Welcome to the heart of strategic real estate success, the mastery of request analysis and trends. In this chapter, we dive deep into the currents of the real estate ocean, where perceptive navigation can make the difference between success and recession.

1. Decoding Market Dynamics

unleash the secrets behind request oscillations, demand-force dynamics, and profitable pointers. Learn to read the subtle signals that shape real estate trends. With this knowledge, you will be equipped to make informed opinions, situating yourself as a perceptive professional in a dynamic request.

2. Trendspotting 101

Come a trendspotter extraordinaire as we anatomize arising patterns and shifts in buyer preferences. From the rise of sustainable living to the impact of technological advancements, we'll explore how trends shape the real estate geography. Stay ahead of the wind and influence trends to your advantage, creating openings where others see challenges.

3. Data-Driven Decision Making

In the age of information, data is mightiness'. Discover how to harness the wealth of data available to make strategic opinions. From comprehensive request reports to prophetic analytics, we'll guide you in exercising data-driven perceptivity to upgrade your investment strategies and maximize returns.

 The keys to unleashing real estate success are in your hands, and your trip to learning request analysis and trends starts now. Prepare yourself for a transformative disquisition of the request's intricate cotillion.

CHAPTER 3

Effective Negotiation Strategies for Success

Welcome to the art of the deal where we unveil the essential chops and strategies that set top-league real estate professionals piecemeal. As you immerse yourself in the world of accommodations, prepare to upgrade your prowess and elevate your success in the competitive arena.

1. The Psychology of Negotiation

Claw into the psychology that underlies successful accommodations. Understand the motives and feelings driving both parties and learn to navigate the delicate balance between fierceness and empathy. learning the cerebral nuances of concession is the key to forging mutually salutary agreements.

2. Tactical Communication Techniques

Communication is the bedrock of effective concession. Explore conclusive communication ways, active listening chops, and the power of strategic silence. Discover how to articulate your value proposition persuasively and make fellowship with guests, creating a foundation for fruitful accommodations.

3. Overcoming Obstacles and Deadlocks

In the intricate cotillion of concession, obstacles are ineluctable. Gain perceptivity into feting and prostrating common hurdles, from pricing controversies to contract contingencies. Learn to transfigure gridlocks into openings, ensuring that accommodations progress easily toward a successful conclusion.

 As you navigate the world of concession, fantasize about yourself as a master strategist. Each commerce is an oil for you to paint a picture of success. Embrace the art, upgrade your chops, and let concession come to your hand strength.

CHAPTER 4

Building a Profitable Property Portfolio

Step into the realm of wealth creation through strategic property accession. In this vital chapter, we unravel the complications of erecting a profitable property portfolio – a crucial corner for any Real Estate Wealthcraft Professional.

1. Crafting Your Investment Strategy

Define your investment pretensions and chart a strategic course for your portfolio. Whether you aspire for steady rental income, robust capital appreciation, or a balanced blend of both, we guide you through the process of acclimatizing an investment strategy that aligns with your objectives.

2. Identifying Prime Investment Opportunities

Navigate the different geography of real estate openings, from domestic and marketable parcels to arising requests and niche parts. Learn to identify high investment openings, conduct thorough due industriousness, and seize the right deals at the right time.

3. Risk Mitigation and Diversification

Structure wealth requires not just occasion recognition but also threat operation. Explore ways to alleviate pitfalls and guard your portfolio against request oscillations. Understand the power of diversification and how to produce a flexible portfolio that withstands profitable misgivings.

As you embark on the trip of erecting your property portfolio, fantasize about yourself as a strategic mastermind, opting for each piece to construct a masterpiece. Get ready to turn bournes into palpable means. Your portfolio, your heritage, awaits.

CHAPTER 5

Navigating Legalities in Real Estate Transactions

Drink to the anchor of ethical and fairly sound real estate practices. In this chapter, we claw into the complications of navigating lawfulness in real estate deals, ensuring your professional trip isn't only successful but also erected on a foundation of integrity.

1. Legal Frameworks Unveiled

Gain a comprehensive understanding of the legal fabrics that govern real estate deals. From property rights to contractual scores, we explore the legal geography that shapes your liabilities as a Real Estate Wealthcraft Professional. Be equipped with the knowledge to navigate legal complications with confidence.

2. Due Diligence Essentials

Explore the art of due industriousness – a pivotal aspect of legal compliance in real estate. Uncover the way to conduct thorough property assessments, title quests, and exposure reviews. Learn how scrupulous due industriousness not only safeguards your guests but also enhances your character as a secure professional.

3. Ethical Practices and Professional Conduct

Claw into the ethical considerations that bolster every successful real estate sale. Understand the significance of translucency, fairness, and adherence to professional canons of conduct. Elevate your practice by cultivating a character for integrity, icing long-term success in the dynamic world of real estate.

As you navigate the legal geography, you won't only be a transactional expert but as a guardian of ethical norms. Your commitment to legal industriousness is the bedrock of enduring success in real estate. Let this chapter be your companion to a professional trip erected on legitimacy, ethics, and excellence.

CHAPTER 6

The Art of Customer Relationship Management

Step into the realm where success isn't just measured in deals but in enduring connections. This chapter unravels the art of customer relationship operation – a foundation in the edifice of a Real Estate Wealthcraft Professional's success.

1. Understanding Client Needs

Embark on a trip to understand the different requirements and bournes of your guests. Learn to hear laboriously, ask perceptive questions, and discern the subtle cues that guide you in acclimatizing your services to meet and exceed their prospects. Your capability to understand customer requirements is the key to fostering lasting connections.

2. Effective Communication Strategies

Communication is the lifeblood of customer connections. Explore strategies to articulate complex real estate generalities in a clear and accessible manner. From timely updates to visionary communication during accommodations, we claw into the nuances that ensure your guests are informed and confident throughout the process.

3. Building Trust and Credibility

Trust is the currency of real estate. Discover the rudiments that contribute to erecting trust and credibility with your guests. From transparent communication to demonstrating moxie, we guide you in cultivating a character that precedes you – one of trust, professionalism, and responsibility.

As you immerse yourself in the art of customer relationship operation (CRM), see each customer commerce as an occasion to produce a lasting connection. Your capability to make and nurture connections transcends individual deals, laying the roots for a flourishing real estate career. The customer

connections you forge moment
are the foundation of your
success hereafter.

CHAPTER 7

Innovative Marketing Techniques for Realtors

Step into the dynamic world of real estate marketing, where invention is the key to visibility and success. This chapter unveils a comprehensive companion to innovative marketing ways acclimatized for forward-allowing Realtors.

1. Crafting Your Unique Brand

Discover the power of branding and how it can set you piecemeal in a crowded request. Learn to define your unique value proposition, creating a brand that resonates with your target followership. Your brand is further than a totem – it's a pledge and a representation of your professional identity.

2. Digital Domains and Online Presence

Navigate the digital geography with confidence. From creating an engaging website to learning social media platforms, explore how to establish a strong online presence. influence the digital realm to connect with guests, showcase your rosters, and place yourself as a study leader in the real estate space.

3. Creative Content Strategies

Content is king, and creativity is its crown. Uncover the secrets of casting compelling content that captivates your followership. From blog posts and vids to virtual tenures, we explore different content strategies that not only showcase your parcels but also establish you as a knowledgeable and engaging Realtor.

 As you claw into the realm of innovative marketing in this chapter, you aren't just a Realtor but also a marketing maestro. Your capability to work in innovative ways won't only enhance your visibility but also solidify your position as a slice-edge professional in the competitive real estate geography. Embrace creativity, technology, and strategic marketing for unequaled success.

CHAPTER 8

Sustainable Success Balancing Ethics and Profitability

Welcome to the climaxing chapter of your trip as a Real Estate Wealthcraft Professional. In this vital chapter, we explore the delicate balance between ethics and profitability – a balance that defines not only your success but also the heritage you leave in the world of real estate.

1. The Ethical Compass

Claw into the ethical considerations that bolster every decision and action in the real estate profession. Understand the significance of integrity, translucency, and a commitment to ethical conduct. Your ethical compass isn't just a companion it's the foundation of sustainable success.

2. Creating Win-Win Scripts

Explore the art of concession and deal-making that prioritizes mutually salutary issues. Learn to produce palm-palm scripts where both you and your guests walk down satisfied. Sustainable success is erected on connections and positive gests, fostering reprise business and referrals.

3. Long-Term Vision and Adaptability

Success isn't just about the present – it's about the enduring heritage you produce. Develop a long-term vision for your real estate career, considering request trends, customer requirements, and evolving assiduity dynamics. Embrace rigidity as a crucial particularity, ensuring you stay ahead in a dynamic and ever-changing terrain.

As you navigate the path of sustainable success, place yourself not just as a successful professional but as a slave of ethical practices. Your commitment to a balance between ethics and profitability sets the stage for a career that not only thrives in the present but leaves a continuing impact. The trip to sustainable success awaits, and you're poised to crop as a lamp of excellence in the world of Real Estate Wealthcraft.

CHAPTER 9

Lifelong Learning and Professional Development

Welcome to the chapter that marks the morning of a commitment to nonstop growth and excellence. In the ever-evolving geography of real estate, embracing lifelong literacy and professional development isn't just a choice – it's a necessity for sustained success.

1. The Dynamic Learning Curve

Embark on a trip of nonstop literacy, fetching that the real estate assiduity is a dynamic geography with ever-shifting trends and regulations. Explore the significance of staying informed about request updates, arising technologies, and evolving consumer preferences.

2. Embracing New Technologies

The digital period has changed the way real estate professionals operate. Dive into the realm of prop-tech, virtual reality tenures, and data analytics. Understand how embracing new technologies can enhance your effectiveness, give innovative results to guests, and position you as a tech-smart leader in the field.

3. Networking and Industry Involvement

Your professional network is a precious asset. Learn the art of effective networking within the real estate assiduity and related sectors. Explore openings to engage with professional associations, attend conferences, and share in assiduity events.

Active involvement not only expands your knowledge base but also opens doors to collaborations and hookups.

As you immerse yourself in the lifelong literacy trip in this chapter, you aren't a static professional but a dynamic force in the real estate geography. Embrace each literacy occasion as a stepping gravestone toward mastery. The commitment to nonstop enhancement is the secret component that propels successful real estate professionals toward enduring excellence. Let this chapter be your companion as you embark on a path of lifelong literacy and professional development. The trip is ongoing, and the possibilities for growth are measurable.

CONCLUSION

Throughout these chapters, we have navigated the foundations, request dynamics, concession strategies, portfolio structure, legal complications, customer connections, innovative marketing, and the delicate balance between ethics and profitability. Each hand contributes to the holistic skill set needed for success in the ever-evolving world of real estate.

In concluding our disquisition into the complications of outstripping as a Real Estate

Wealthcraft Professional, we reflect upon the multifaceted trip you've accepted. This comprehensive companion has sought to equip you not only with the practical chops necessary for success but also with the mindset and ethical foundation pivotal for sustained excellence.

As you now stand at the capstone of this perceptive passage, fantasize yourself not simply as a real estate professional but as a maestro of the craft – a Wealthcraft Professional who navigates the complications of the request with wit, negotiates with finesse, builds portfolios with perfection, and fosters enduring connections through ethical practices.

Flashback, the world of real estate isn't stationary, and your commitment to lifelong literacy and rigidity is the linchpin for uninterrupted success. Embrace change, harness invention, and stay ahead of assiduity trends to remain at the van of this dynamic field.

As a Real Estate Wealthcraft Professional, your trip will be characterized not only by fiscal substance but by a heritage of integrity, trust, and customer satisfaction. As you forge ahead, may the principles and strategies reprised in this companion serve as a loyal compass, guiding you through the ever-evolving geography of real estate.

This isn't the end but the morning of a career marked by excellence, ethical conduct, and a commitment to lifelong literacy. The oil is yours to paint, the openings are bottomless, and the world of real estate awaits your masterful touch. Go forth with confidence, for you're now equipped to excel as a true handworker in the craft of Real Estate Wealthcraft.

www.ingramcontent.com/pod-product-compliance
Lightning Source LLC
Chambersburg PA
CBHW062301290526
45794CB00006B/2645